WHAT YOUR BIRD NEEDS

By Liz Palika

A Dorling Kindersley Book

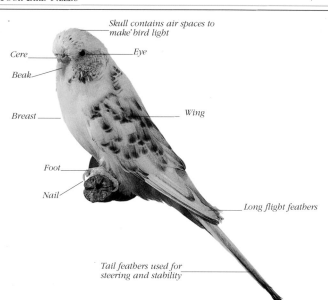

Skull contains air spaces to make bird light

Cere

Eye

Beak

Breast

Wing

Foot

Nail

Long flight feathers

Tail feathers used for steering and stability

WHAT YOUR BIRD NEEDS

	Less	1	2	3	4	5	More
Time commitment					✓		
Exercise		✓					
Play time			✓				
Space requirements		✓					
Grooming		✓					
Feeding			✓				
Cleaning up				✓			
Life span				✓			
Good with kids 5 to 10		✓					
Good with kids 10 and over			✓				

CONTENTS

FOREWORD BY BRUCE FOGLE, DVM

Believe it or not, even budgies live in wild habitats. The next time you're in Australia, look for flocks of them in the trees.

In the first book I ever wrote, *Pets and their People*, the illustrator Lalla Ward made a marvelous sketch of my mother, knitting, with a budgie nestled in her hair. Unfortunately, it never ended up in the book. I do not know why the publisher did not used that illustration, because it captured the mutual relationship between these two individuals. My mother nurtured George, her blue budgie, while George thought of her as good nesting material.

George was not our first family budgie. As well as dogs, cats, and fish, my father made sure we always had birds in our home. (No wonder I ended up as a veterinarian!) Early memories from my childhood are of Mickey, another budgie, shouting, or yelling, or possibly swearing. He must have idolized my mother. He certainly paid more attention to mimicking her than to anyone else.

Why, you might ask, would a reasonably sensible mother with 2.3 kids and a station wagon outside bother with speaking to a budgie or letting one nest in her hair? The answer is she could not help it. She was one of life's natural care givers. And my conclusion from thirty years of clinical veterinary practice is that pet owners are the more nurturing part of society; that caring for birds, in our homes or in our backyards, is simply a manifestation of the satisfaction we get from caring for other living things.

If we are going to care for birds, we should do so well. That involves understanding their physical, environmental, and emotional needs. I am happy to say my family always had groups of birds, an essential for gregariously sociable species like budgies if they are to be kept in as natural a state as possible. To me, a mirror is not a reasonable budgie substitute. If you have only one budgie, you are the budgie substitute and you should plan to do what my mother intuitively did – open the cage and allow your budgie the freedom to choose, safely, what he wants to do. (Do not, as my mother did, frequently go outdoors, forgetting that your budgie is nesting in your beehive hairdo!)

While budgies are still the most popular birds we keep as pets. cockatiels are rising in popularity. Canaries and finches, which have always enchanted us with their songs, are also becoming popular pets. And captive-bred large parrots are starting to become available, as well.

I say "captive-bred" because big, long-lived birds like macaws, Mexican redheaded parrots, and African greys have always been available, but until recently they were trapped in their native habitats. These terrified, wild creatures spent the rest of their lives trying to escape, and the ones that did often found themselves in hostile climates that they could not survive in. Fortunately, these beautiful, intelligent birds are now being bred to be pets. They make calmer, happier companions, and you have the satisfaction of knowing that no wild animal was trapped to become your pet.

As we learn more about these birds, what they need, and just how smart they are, we realize that keeping them alone in cages with nothing but seeds to eat and not much to do is about the worst way to keep a pet bird. It invites all sorts of health and emotional problems.

Getting off to the right start with your birds is the best preventive medicine I can suggest. This little book helps set you on the right course toward what I hope will be a fruitful and mutually rewarding relationship with your bird.

We are now discovering that birds are smarter and more sociable than we had ever imagined.

DESCENDED FROM DINOSAURS

The most ancient fossil known to be that of a bird is about 150 to 160 million years old – from the Jurassic period – and was found in a limestone quarry in Germany. The fossil, which includes feather imprints, is of Archaepteryx, an animal the size of today's crows that looks to be half reptile and half bird – as we know birds and reptiles today. The theory that birds are descended from dinosaurs has been (and still is) greatly debated, but as finds like this one are studied, it appears to be correct.

Birds today are found all over the world in a wide variety of habitats. Birds are living and nesting in mountainous terrains, on cliff sides, rainforests, grasslands, forests, savannas, and even deserts. Birds found all over the world share some common characteristics, including feathers, reproduction by laying eggs, the ability to fly (with a very few exceptions), and a unique skeletal structure that is different from mammals.

In the wild, most birds live in flocks. They spend their days calling to one another to locate food, warn of predators, and simply to confirm that their flockmates are nearby. These are called contact calls, and our domestic birds also make them. Your bird will be reassured to know that her flock – that's you and your family – are near.

DOMESTICATING BIRDS

Birds have been kept as pets for thousands of years. The first recorded bird keeper was Queen Hatshepsut of Egypt. In 1500 BCE she sponsored an expedition to collect hawks and falcons for the royal zoo. Alexander the Great kept birds, including peacocks, parrots, and parakeets. Keeping birds was popular throughout European history and many people kept aviaries full of birds. During the peak of the Roman Empire's glory, talking parrots were the ultimate status symbols.

Although songbirds were popular for their lovely music, and parrots for their ability to mimic human speech, hawks and other birds of prey were often used as partners on the hunt. Artwork from many ages in history shows a hunter mounted on horseback, with a dog (or dogs) running alongside and a hooded hawk or falcon perched on one arm. Although these birds were status symbols and their ownership was often limited to the aristocracy, trained birds of prey also helped provide meat for the table.

Today bird ownership is not limited to any particular class of people, and in fact, the number of people who own birds is growing fast. In recent years we've also learned that birds are much smarter and much more social than we had imagined. Recent studies at the University of Arizona suggest some species of parrots may be as smart as chimpanzees or dolphins!

Wild birds face a number of threats today, including habitat loss, pollution, disease, food availability, and predation by natural predators and domesticated pets. Many wild species have been tamed so that we can enjoy them in our homes, but it's important to leave the wild birds in the wild. Wild-caught birds are terrified, confused animals, and often become aggressive or withdrawn as a result. Always buy captive-bred birds. These are birds that were born and raised to be pets, and they will be better companions for you.

Birds in the wild live in social groups. A bird alone in a cage, with no companions and little human interaction, will be miserable.

THE CAGE

The most important thing you need for
your bird before you bring him home is his
cage. When it comes to cages, bigger is always
better. The cage will be your bird's home and must be the
right type, style, and size so that your bird is relatively stress-
free and comfortable. It must also be secure, so he cannot escape.
Different kinds of birds need different kinds of cages. Here I'll
concentrate on some of the most popular species: budgies (also
known as parakeets), canaries, finches, and cockatiels. If you're
considering a large parrot, you'll need a much bigger cage than the
ones I'll describe here.

BUDGIES

Budgies like to move around and do well with a cage that is tall as
well as wide. A good size cage would be 20 inches long, 16 inches
wide and 24 inches tall. Medium-weight bars should be spaced no
wider than 7/16 of an inch apart, but 3/8 of an inch apart is better.

CANARIES AND FINCHES

These small birds like to fly, so look for a cage that is wider than it is
tall. Thirty inches long by 16 inches wide by 20 inches tall is fine for
a pair of birds. The cage bars can be relatively lightweight, and
should be spaced 3/8 to 7/16 of an inch apart.

COCKATIELS AND LOVEBIRDS

A cage 24 inches square is fine for one of these birds (make sure
your cockatiel will have room to sit on a perch without crushing his
high crest on the top or his long tail on the bottom). Medium-weight
bars spaced 1/2 to 5/8 of an inch apart are fine.

Stick with a square or rectangular cage for all birds. This shape gives
the bird more room to move, plus these cages are safer for your bird.
While round cages and the fancy ones that look like little palaces
sure are pretty, each of those little nooks, crannies, and ornaments on
a fancy cage take away flight space or add connecting edges of wire
where your bird could catch a foot, a wing tip, or even his head. In
addition, the simpler the cage, the easier it is to clean.

The cage doors are very important, because many birds are escape artists – especially when you're at work and the bird is bored. The door must be large enough so that you can bring your bird out and put him away safely, with a minimum of hassle. The door must also fit the cage securely and have a good latch, or a place where you can fasten it open with a clip. For larger birds that are prone to escaping, you might even want to use a small padlock to keep the door closed.

Most cages have a sliding bottom tray you can pull out to clean. This should be easy to use yet still be secure. Make sure there are no gaps large enough for your bird to escape through.

When choosing a cage, look at it from several different aspects. It should be simple yet attractive, so you are comfortable with it in your home. It should be large enough for your bird, with appropriate spacing of the wire bars. It should be relatively easy to clean, the door should be secure, and your bird should feel comfortable and secure inside it.

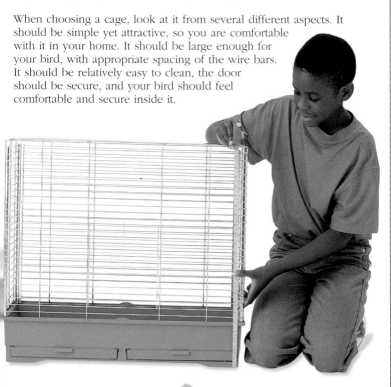

FURNISHING THE CAGE

The cage will need furnishings, so while you're out shopping, bring this shopping list with you.

PERCHES

Your bird will spend most of his life standing on his feet, so good perches are really important. Supply a variety of perches of different sizes so that your bird's feet can move and grip differently throughout the day. Wooden dowels are fine, but natural tree branches are better for variety. A perch is the right diameter when your bird's toenails don't go all the way around it. Ideally, the tips of the nails should touch the perch about two-thirds of the way around. Finches and canaries need perches that are 3/8 to 1/2 inch in diameter. Budgies need perches 1/2 to 3/4 inch in diameter. Cockatiels need 3/4-inch perches.

DISHES

The food and water dishes should be easy to clean, sturdy, and the appropriate size for your bird. Obviously, a finch will not need a bowl big enough for an Amazon parrot, and the parrot could destroy the finch's small plastic bowl. Make sure the bowl fits into the slot built into the cage, or use perches with fastenings for bowls.

GROOMING SUPPLIES

These will vary depending upon what type of bird you get, but all will need nail clippers, a sharp pair of scissors, a spray bottle for misting, and a bird bath. You can use an ordinary plant mister and a plastic dish for your bird's bath and shower, but they must be put aside especially for the bird and not used for anything else. So buy new ones now.

NEST BOX

Most small birds, especially finches, like a hiding place. Small wicker or wooden houses can be fastened inside the cage towards the top. Make sure the box you choose is easily cleaned.

CAGE COVER

A cage cover will protect your bird from drafts, which is important. It also signals to your bird that this is bedtime and he's expected to be quiet. You can buy a special cover if you can find one to fit the cage, but an old sheet or pillowcase will work just as well.

TOYS

Birds need things in their cage to stimulate their minds and bodies. Just make sure they are appropriate to the type of bird you're bringing home. Budgies and finches will appreciate small, lightweight toys and tiny mirrors. Larger birds like toys they can manipulate with their beak, tongue, and feet. Most parrot species, including budgies and cockatiels, will chew their toys mercilessly, so choose items made from wood or hardened plastic.

MORE INFORMATION

Look for a book or two on the particular type of bird you're bringing home, as well as a more detailed book about general bird care. If you have an especially intelligent species, such as an African grey or a macaw, you may want to pick up a book on bird training. The more you know, the fewer mistakes you will make; your bird will certainly appreciate it!

SKIP THE SANDPAPER

It was once thought that sandpaper covers on a bird's perch and lining the bottom of the cage were a good idea to help keep a bird's nails trimmed. We now know better. Sandpaper scratches your poor bird's feet, and is never a good idea for any bird. Try one concrete perch to give your bird a head start on grooming his beak and nails (you'll still have to trim the nails regularly), and line the bottom of the cage with sheets of newspaper that you change every day.

A PLACE TO PLAY

Playgyms and parrot playgrounds are special playgrounds made just for your bird. They are a great way for your bird to get out of his cage and do something interesting and entertaining. Playgyms engage your bird's body and his mind – an important combination for such a social, intelligent animal. Most are commercially produced for specific types of birds and are designed so that they can be set on a table or attached to a cage.

Before you buy a playgym, decide what kind will be best for your bird. Budgies and cockatiels, if their wings are clipped, can play on the smaller sets made for their size, as can lovebirds and small conures. The larger birds, especially the parrots, will need a sturdier playgym made to withstand their powerful beaks.

Most playgyms have vertical and horizontal perches, bars or dowels that encourage climbing. Most of the time there are perches or bars of different diameters, and often the perches are made of different things, even natural branches, for variety and for the bird's

NOT FOR SONGBIRDS

The smallest birds, especially canaries and finches and other birds that are not in the parrot family, don't need a playgym. They can get enough exercise in their roomy cage with a few small toys. Plus, their wings are not usually clipped, so they could simply fly away from the playgym.

exploration. Many have slanted bars that are a little more difficult for the bird to climb but offer a good challenge. Some have ramps or little staircases for the bird to hop up. Most also have toys for the bird to explore, play with, and even chew up. You should be able to replace the destroyed toys with new ones.

When choosing a playgym, choose one that will work for you (attached to a cage or set on a table) and choose one appropriate to your size bird. Make sure, too, that it is easily cleaned, either with a pull-out tray or designed so it is simply easy to wash.

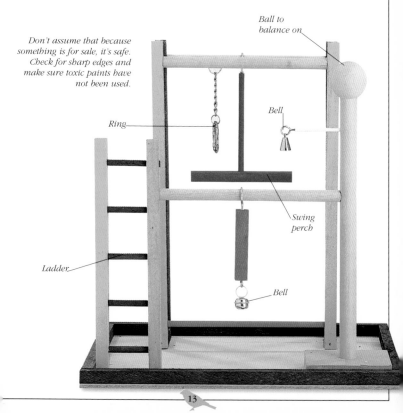

Don't assume that because something is for sale, it's safe. Check for sharp edges and make sure toxic paints have not been used.

Ball to balance on

Ring

Bell

Swing perch

Ladder

Bell

THE PERFECT SPOT

Where should you place
your bird's cage? There are
several things to think about when
you're deciding where to put it.

First of all, most birds are happiest when
they're part of the family. Birds don't like to be
alone too much and may pout, refuse to eat, and
could even get angry and aggressive when they're not getting enough
attention. So place the cage where people normally gather in the
house. The family room, a large kitchen, or a playroom are good.

NOT TOO MUCH NOISE

Make sure the cage is not in a place where the volume is always (or
often) turned up high. If the kids have their own television and
boom box in the family room and often turn up the volume, don't
put the bird's cage in that room. Instead, place his cage in the room
where mom and dad hang out and watch television at a lower
volume.

NO TEMPERATURE EXTREMES

Birds are sensitive to changes of temperature and drafts, so don't put
the cage right in front of a door, a heating or air conditioning vent, or
a window. Make sure your bird won't be stuck in the sun for hours
with no place to cool down. Most birds feel more secure if at least
one side of their cage is protected, so put the cage up against one
wall or in the corner of a room.

IS IT CONVENIENT FOR YOU?

Make sure you are going to be comfortable where the bird cage is
located. Is the bird going to disrupt your phone calls? Will he make
visitors uncomfortable? How about noise; if he sings (or screams),
will he bother the neighbors? Is this spot easily cleaned? Are his
feathers (and feces) going to fall on your prized Persian rug or the
carved chair you inherited from your grandmother?

Once you have a location picked out, make sure there is nothing the
bird can reach and destroy within beak range. Birds in the parrot

family can be very destructive, so make sure curtains, wall paper, electrical cords, and picture frames are out of reach.

USE A PLAYGYM TO CARRY YOUR BIRD AROUND

Once you decide on a location for the cage, try not move it. Each move will upset your bird. If you wish to bring him with you from room to room (which most birds enjoy), carry him on his playgym or a freestanding perch and let his cage stay where it is.

A free-standing perch is just a stand with a base to catch droppings and a perch or two with a food and water cup. Most birds (with clipped wings) quickly learn to stay on the perch, and this can be carried from room to room so your bird can spend time with you without having to be in your hands or on your shoulder.

Place the cage at eye level if you can, so you can easily talk to your bird and feed him from your hand.

BRINGING YOUR BIRD HOME

Make sure you have a carrier to bring your bird home in. Never attempt to carry a bird home, even in the car, without some kind of a carrier. A small cardboard box could work, or a small or midsize cat carrier. Most places where you buy a bird will give you a small carrier with the bird.

At home, with the cage already set up, check to make sure all of the doors and windows of your house are closed, then transfer the bird from his carrier to his cage. You may be able to simply open the carrier and hold it up to the opened cage door, letting your bird move into the cage on his own. This is really the best way, so try to be patient and let your bird move in on his own. If that won't work, tilt the carrier a bit, so your bird will find it easier to slide out into the cage than to hang on in the carrier. Resist the urge to tap on the carrier or shake it; your bird is probably scared, and you don't want to scare him more.

START OUT SLOW

For the first two days, leave your bird in his cage and let him get used to his new home. He will explore his cage, discover his food and water, and watch what's going on around him. Let him observe people moving around in a fairly normal routine. Make sure he's protected from your other pets, especially the dog, the cat, and the ferret – all predators to a bird.

During these first two days, don't invite friends, neighbors, and relatives over to meet your new bird. It's too much too soon. Make sure your children understand they need to be quiet – with no rough play or loud noises – for the first few days. Keep the television and stereo volumes fairly low, too, and don't get the vacuum cleaner out for a few days.

Talk to your new bird often in a quiet, soft but happy tone of voice, but don't get in your bird's face while you talk. If your bird starts beating his wings against the bars of his cage, you are too close. Stand a few feet away and speak, or talk as you walk through the room where his cage is set up.

After the first two days, if your bird is eating well and doesn't appear startled at the things going on around him, start gradually (over several days) moving back to a normal routine. The volume of the television can go back up and your kids' friends can come back over to play. After all, your bird is going to be living with your household as it is; he needs to get used to it.

If the carrier will fit all the way inside the cage, simply place it on the cage floor and let your bird come out on his own.

AVIAN NUTRITION

When it comes to their food, all birds are not alike. Some birds in the wild prefer seeds, while others prefer only insects, fruits. Some birds eat while others eat just about anything. However, most birds digest their food in much the same manner. The food that is eaten must be broken down into simpler chemical forms, and in birds that process begins in the crop. The crop is a pouch located at the base of the esophagus. Food passes from the crop to the first part of the stomach, where it is mixed with digestive juices. Then it moves to the second part of the stomach, where it is ground up with the help of grit, gravel, or sand that the bird has swallowed. The food then moves into the intestinal tract, where nutrients are absorbed into the body and wastes are excreted.

Good nutrition is made up of several important components, which I've listed below. All of these must be present in your bird's diet.

○ **Vitamins** are organic compounds that affect the metabolism of food, growth, reproduction, and a thousand other body processes.

○ **Minerals** are inorganic compounds that work in conjunction with other minerals, vitamins, amino acids, or enzymes.

○ **Amino acids** are found in proteins, and also help the body metabolize proteins. They are also needed for growth, healing, and other body processes.

○ **Proteins** can be complete or incomplete. Complete proteins have all the amino acids needed for good health,

and can be found in eggs, red meats, fish, and dairy products. Incomplete proteins are still good food, but contain only some of the needed amino acids. These can be found in beans, soybeans, nuts, grains, and potatoes.

○ **Enzymes** are protein-based chemicals found in every cell of the body. They work to cause biochemical reactions that affect metabolism. Most work with a co-enzyme, usually a vitamin.

○ **Fats** help metabolize the fat-soluble vitamins D, E, and K. Fats are also a source of energy.

○ **Carbohydrates** are sugars and starches used by the body as fuel.

WHAT DO BIRDS EAT?

How do you know what particular foods a bird might eat? The shape of the bird's beak gives us a few clues. For example, the hummingbird's long, narrow beak shows us those birds eat (or drink) nectar. Birds with cone-shaped beaks are primarily seed eaters (sparrows, finches, cardinals, canaries, and pigeons). Birds with long, thin beaks are primarily insect eaters (wrens, warblers, vireos, mockingbirds, and titmice). Birds with strong hooked beaks need them for hard-to-eat foods. Parrots use their strong beaks for fruits and nuts, while birds of prey (falcons, hawks, eagles) use their sharp beaks to eat their prey.

In the past we have had a tendency to keep birds that could survive on seeds, since seeds were easy for us to provide. Today, however, we have access to a variety of food items, including commercially prepared foods, plus we know a lot more about nutrition. One of the things we've learned is that birds do not really thrive on a seed-only diet. Seeds lack a lot of things birds need, including some amino acids and important vitamins and minerals. As we learn more, we can provide our pet birds with a much better, and often more natural, diet.

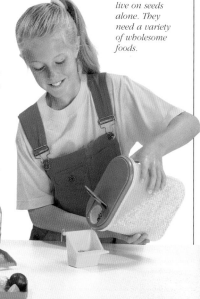

Birds do not live on seeds alone. They need a variety of wholesome foods.

The type of bird you have obviously affects what foods he must eat. Your bird's age is also important in deciding what he needs. A young, rapidly growing bird has different nutritional needs than an adult, for example. Whether or not your bird is part of a breeding program affects his (or her) nutritional needs, as does the bird's activity level, state of health, and stress levels. All of these things must be taken into consideration when you're feeding your bird.

WHAT DO BIRDS EAT?

There is no one food right for every bird. Birds should eat as varied a diet as possible so that all of their nutritional needs are met. In the wild, a bird eating seeds is not going to eat just one type of seed. Instead, that bird will eat seeds from a variety of plants and will eat unripe seeds as well as ripe seeds. As the bird eats those seeds, he will probably also pick up some nectar, some pollen and a few insects. In addition, his diet will vary through the seasons, depending on what foods are available.

Our goal is to provide our birds with the best diet we can. So what can we feed them? Here are some foods that are good for most birds:

GRAINS

This includes oats, wheat, barley, and grain products. Whole grain breads, pastas, rice, and cereals are all nutritious foods. Grain products are a good source of vitamins, minerals, fiber, proteins, and carbohydrates.

SEEDS

Some common seeds include millet, canary grass, flax, hemp, white lettuce, milo, niger, safflower, sunflower, and rape seeds. Safflower and sunflower seeds are high in oil, fat, and calories. Seeds can be good nutrition, but can not supply all of your bird's nutritional needs.

FRESH VEGETABLES

Vegetables supply a wide range of vitamins, minerals, and trace elements, and should be a part of every bird's diet. Some good vegetables include grated or chopped carrots, grated or chopped broccoli, collard greens, kale, grated or chopped squash, sweet potato, tomatoes, and zucchini. Fresh sprouts (such as broccoli or alfalfa) are also good food, but they must be absolutely fresh.

Fresh Fruits

Some good fresh fruits include apple, banana, strawberry, cantaloupe, grapes, berries, and other melons. Fruits supply many vitamins and minerals, but feed judiciously because too many fresh fruits could cause loose stools.

Nuts

Nuts are very nutritious, and can include shelled walnuts, almonds, Brazil nuts, and peanuts. Smaller birds like finches will eat finely chopped nuts, while the hooked bill birds will relish cracking the nuts themselves.

Meat and Insects

Meats add protein to the bird's diet, and although most birds are not primarily meat-eaters, many will accept meat as a treat or as a smaller part of their diet. Cooked chicken or beef, finely chopped, can be added in very small amounts to most diets. Commercially raised insects such as mealworms, waxworms, and crickets can be offered to most birds as a treat or as a small part of their diet.

Eggs

Hardboiled, mashed chicken eggs are good nutrition and can be added to the diets of most birds. Crushed eggshells are a good source of grit for the digestive system.

Commercial Pelleted Bird Foods

Commercial pelleted bird foods can be very good nutrition for your bird if (and only if) the commercial food is of good quality and is made from high-quality ingredients. These foods were designed to provide complete and balanced nutrition for your bird. Some birds will accept these foods quite readily, while others resist eating them. Many bird breeders start their young birds on commercial foods right from the beginning, so there is no problem getting them to eat.

Water

Your bird should always have fresh water in his cage. Make sure the water dish is positioned so that a perch is not above it; if one is, the bowl will quickly be fouled with feces. If the water is dirty, change it right away.

WHAT'S GOOD FOR YOUR BIRD?

BUDGIES

A varied seed mixture that includes canary grass seed, millet, chopped oats, anise, rape seeds, flax, and milo is fine. Commercial pellet foods are also good. Add a few fruits and vegetables every day. A tiny bit of meat and a few insects can add variety.

CANARIES

A varied seed diet that includes canola seeds, rape, oats, niger, hemp, and flax is high in carbohydrates and protein – both of which are important to this species. Canary grass seeds, millet, and white lettuce seeds are also good. Add some fruits and vegetables for variety. Canaries have a very fast metabolism and eat one-fourth their weight every day, so keep the food cups full!

COCKATIELS

These birds need a varied diet that includes seeds, grain products (whole grain breads or pastas), cereal, and rice cakes, as well as fresh fruits and vegetables. Commercial pelleted foods are also good. A bit of meat and some insects will add variety.

FINCHES

Finches are seed eaters and will eat millet, niger, rape seed, hemp,

THE NITTY GRITTY

Grit is a mixture of sand, tiny pieces of gravel and sometimes ground oyster shell. Grit in the second part of the bird's stomach helps him grind up his food, especially hard seeds and nuts. This enables the bird to digest his food. Experts agree that canaries and finches need grit and should have a small dish of it in their cage. They also agree that most large birds, including Amazon parrots and macaws, do not need grit, since these birds break up their food and rarely eat the tiny, hard seeds that small birds eat. Experts don't agree as to whether budgies, cockatiels, conures, and other medium-size birds need grit. Most do agree, however, that offering these bird a dish of grit once a week as supplementation will not hurt them.

and canary grass seed. Flax seed, anise, and poppy seeds are also good. Some grated carrot, finely chopped greens, and a piece of apple are good treats.

WHAT ABOUT SUPPLEMENTS?

Deciding whether or not to add supplements to your bird's food, or what supplements to add, is difficult. Too much of any particular supplement might endanger your bird's health, while too little of a particular nutrient might do the same thing. So what should you do?

First of all, concentrate on feeding the best diet you can. Then, and only then, think about what supplement you want to feed and why – is it necessary for your bird's good health? Adding a supplement to any diet should not disrupt the balance of the food. In addition, any supplement should be given only according to the manufacturer's directions, so read the label carefully!

If you are feeding a seed mixture with fruits and vegetables added, it will probably be safe to feed a vitamin and mineral supplement appropriate to your bird's species. If you are feeding a good quality commercial pelleted bird food only, the vitamin and mineral supplement probably isn't needed.

If your bird is recovering from an injury or illness, a supplement might be needed to help him regain optimum health, but talk to your veterinarian before adding any special supplements. Again, the best thing for your bird is a good, balanced diet every day.

CALCIUM AND PHOSPHORUS

Calcium and phosphorus imbalances often show up during breeding season when the female bird (called the hen) must produce enough calcium for her eggs. A cuttlebone in the cage is enough for most birds. However, some birds need more than a bone. If you suspect your bird might have an imbalance, talk to your veterinarian before supplementing her diet. A cuttlebone or mineral block (the kind made specifically for birds) is safe for almost all birds, but too much or improper calcium or mineral supplementation can be deadly.

You can buy a cuttlebone at pet supply stores. They usually come with clips that fasten to the cage.

WHEN TO FEED YOUR BIRD

Birds must be fed every day. Once each day, preferably in the morning (since most birds want to eat when they wake up), the food and water dishes should be pulled from the cage, emptied, washed thoroughly, and refilled. Unlike many mammals, birds do not fast well. Some (finches, canaries, and other small birds) can die after a short period without food. Therefore, set up a routine for feeding and stick to that schedule, because your bird will expect it.

Most birds will eat in the morning and then go back to eat now and then throughout the day. Unless there is a medical reason for it (as instructed by your veterinarian), don't take away the bird's food. Leave food in the dish all day. If the food becomes fouled by feces, take it away, dispose of it, and refill the dish with clean food.

Just because you feed the primary meal in the morning, though, doesn't mean you can't give your bird a snack or two throughout the day. Most bird owners enjoy giving their bird a small snack when they eat their own meals, and there's nothing wrong with this as long as the snack is counted as part of the bird's normal diet. For example, if you feed the bird his seed mixture, veggies, and commercial food in the morning, you may want to give the bird some vegetables at noon and some fruit in the evening as snacks.

At night, before you go to bed, throw away any fresh fruits or vegetables your bird hasn't eaten and give him clean water, but leave his seeds or pellets overnight.

FUN FEEDING

Because of their high metabolism (canaries and finches will eat one quarter of their weight each day!), most wild birds spend a great deal of their day foraging for food. In captivity, of course, food is always in front of them. So what do they do with the rest of the day? Some birds, when bored, will develop bad habits, including destructive chewing, feather picking, or screaming to pass the time. You can help to alleviate boredom by making feeding time more fun and more challenging.

One food dish should always contain a fresh serving of the bird's basic diet – a seed mixture for seed eaters, or commercial pellets – while another dish could be refilled at various times with different foods. One time it might have chopped greens, another time quartered grapes, and another time nuts. A sprig of millet can be hung from a cage bar with a clip so that the bird must maneuver around on the cage side bars to eat it. (Don't make it too easy!) A long stalk of celery with a little peanut butter smeared on it or a broccoli flowerette can also be clamped to a cage bar.

Another fun way to present food is to make your bird a string of food. Use heavy string and a needle. Use the needle to pierce a slice of apple, a chunk of carrot, a slice of banana, a piece of sweet potato, a cherry tomato, or other good foods. Hang the string of food in the cage and watch your bird have fun with it. For larger birds, do the same thing except use a heavy-gauge wire to string the food.

You can also make food fun by stringing some pieces of food along with some toys. Use your imagination, but keep safety in mind. Make sure your bird can't hurt himself with these new foods and toys. You may want to supervise him the first time you introduce something new, just in case.

Wild birds spend most of their time foraging for food, but pet birds get their food presented to them every day. That's why obesity is a real problem in pet birds. Supplement your bird's high-fat seeds with low-fat snacks like fruit and vegetables, measure how much you are feeding each day, and make sure your bird gets plenty of exercise.

INTELLIGENT ANIMALS GET BORED EASILY

All birds are not alike. Some, like
canaries and finches, are small, fast-
moving, and sing lovely songs. Others,
like parrots and macaws, are big, strong,
and loud. Birds are not alike when it comes
to intelligence, either. The smallest birds (again,
canaries and finches) are smart in the things that are
important to them – for example, survival. These birds
are very concerned with becoming someone's lunch and
their instinct to fly away from potential problems is very
strong. Therefore, things like cuddling with their owner, and
learning and performing tricks, is not important to them.

The larger birds are more confident about their ability to protect
themselves from harm and are able to use their native intelligence for
other things, including play. The medium-size birds (budgies,
cockatiels, and smaller conures) have some of both traits. They still
have a strong flight instinct to escape from trouble, but they have the
intelligence and desire to play and socialize.

When an intelligent creature such as a bird is in a cage, boredom
quickly follows. When a bird is bored, he will try to amuse himself.
Sometimes he'll play with his toys, but the same toys seen day after
day can get boring, too, so he may try other things to amuse himself.
He may tear up his perch, if he can, or he may reach through his
cage bars and tear up his cage cover. Bad behaviors such as feather
pulling and screaming are also ways birds cope with boredom.

To alleviate boredom, the smallest birds that are not easily handled,
such as canaries and finches, often do better in pairs. Two birds will
amuse one another and keep each other company. Even budgies
often do better in pairs. However, birds that are more easily handled
(without stress) and more easily trained need to spend time out of
their cage, both to alleviate boredom and also to become better
friends with you.

Before taking your bird out of his cage for playtime and bonding, make sure his wings are clipped so that he cannot escape. I'll explain more about that on page 47.

BIRD PROOFING

It's important to look at your home and the places where your bird will spend time out of his cage. When your bird is out and about with you, you need to make sure he isn't going to destroy things or get himself into trouble. For example, the scrap papers that my cockatiel Pretty Bird is ripping up into tiny pieces right now are papers I gave him. I made sure my desk was clear of important papers before I put Pretty Bird on the desk. There is also nothing within his reach, like curtains or dangling pull cords, when he's sitting on his window perch.

If you routinely place your bird in the same place while he's out of the cage with you, make sure there are no phone cords, electrical cords, electrical outlets, lamps, appliances, important things, knick-knacks, or anything else that is of value or dangerous within reach. Birds are very curious, and their curiosity will get them into trouble if you let it!

The same applies to a freestanding perch or playgym. Because this is often portable, you may set it in different locations. Try to get into the habit of looking at what is within your bird's reach when you set it down. If you put it too close to the drapes, don't get angry when your bird takes a big chunk out of the drapes! He's doing what comes naturally to him – exploring the world around him. If something bad happens, it's your fault that you didn't prevent it from happening.

Smoke from nonstick cookware is toxic to birds. If your bird is routinely kept in or anywhere near the kitchen, give away your nonstick pans. It's a small price to pay for the health of your pet.

OUT OF THE CAGE

Time out of the cage can be spent on the
playgym, or could be spent on a freestanding
perch in the room where you're spending
time. Wherever it is, this is time that is best
spent bonding with your bird – when you can
teach your bird to trust you and to enjoy being
near you. Bonding with your bird is a process; it
takes time. Unlike a puppy, who may love you
within minutes of meeting you, a bird (especially an
adult bird) is much more like a wild animal. This
bird needs to watch you for a while. Then he will begin to trust you
and bond with you.

TIPS TO HELP YOU BOND WITH YOUR BIRD

○ Speak to your bird often using a soft, friendly tone of voice, and move
slowly and quietly around the bird.
○ Hold your bird close to you at about the level of your heart.
○ When stroking your bird, do so gently. If he is stressed by the petting,
stop for a moment and speak gently to him.
○ Offer him a special treat to eat while you're holding him.
○ Don't get angry if your bird bites you; this is his only defense against
things he fears.

As you begin to bond with your bird out of his cage, don't take him
outside of the house or to new places (other than in your home) that
will frighten him. Instead, as he learns to trust you, let him ride on
your hand as you walk from one room to another. Let him see and
hear things around the house. It may be years before he's confident
enough to go outside with you (without being in a carrier), and some
birds are never confident enough or trustworthy enough to do so.

As you work with your bird, keep in mind that birds are secure in a
flock – and in your home, you are your bird's flock. Even if he is
initially wary of you, he really does want to be friends. He just needs

to get over his fear. So take your time, and be patient, gentle, and slow. All your efforts will be worth it when your bird finally decides you're a pretty good friend!

SPENDING MORE TIME OUT

As your bird becomes more comfortable with you and his trust in you builds, he can spend more time out of his cage with you.

You will need to figure out when the best time is for you to bond with your bird. You can bring him out when you're sitting on the sofa watching television, or when you and the children are discussing their day at school. Your bird doesn't have to be the center of attention when you bring him out. He'll be happy just to be with you and the other family members.

However, don't bring your bird out when you are doing things that could be dangerous. Don't bring him out and set him on your shoulder while you're ironing or cooking, for example.

Before you take your bird out of his cage, check that all doors and windows are closed. Don't reply on your memory – check.

FINGER TRAINING YOUR BIRD

One of the most important lessons your bird should learn is to climb on your finger when you ask him to. If your bird tries to act like an escape artist (and they all do at some point), you can get the situation back under control if you can ask him to step down off the curtain rod or picture frame onto your finger. And if he flutters to the floor off your hand, you can ask him to step up on to your finger. Birds do not like to be grabbed (that's too much like a predator-prey situation), but if your bird will step up on your finger you won't have to grab him at all.

After a few days (or even a week) of letting your bird get used to your household, you can teach him the command "up," which means "step up onto my finger." With your fingers together and the back of your hand held towards your bird, index finger up, put your hand in front of your bird. Hold the top of your index finger just slightly higher than the perch your bird is standing on. Tell your bird "Sweetie, up!" If your bird gets on your finger, praise him in a higher than normal tone of voice, but don't get so excited that you scare him off your finger.

If you don't yet have a bird on your finger, gently press your hand against his tummy and tell him again, "Sweetie, up!" (Keep in mind that he has no idea what this word means at this point in his training.) You may have to move your hand in front of your bird several times until he steps on; that's fine. Once he's on, praise him. Practice this several times a day until your bird will step up willingly and readily when you place your hand in front of him and give the "up" command.

If your bird starts beating his wings against the side of the cage and acts frightened when your hand comes near, he may not be ready for this training yet. Give him a little more time to get to know you. Take a week or two and try hand feeding him some special treats so he gets used to your hands being the bearers of good things. Then try this training again.

Once your bird will step up on your fingers (in his cage only right now), move your hand a little so he gets used to the movements of your hand and learns to adjust his balance. Move him from one perch to another on your finger, telling him each time, "Sweetie, up!" and praising him when he accepts the transfers. Take a week or two to practice both of these skills.

When you feel comfortable with your bird on your finger and he's used to you moving your hand, invite him on your finger and bring him out the door of his cage. Make sure you center him sideways and slightly lower than center vertically so that you don't bump his head or his wings, or squash his tail. Birds are quite fragile and a hard bump will hurt! Once he's out, praise him and then turn him around and put him back in, giving him a treat once he's on his perch again. Do this three or four times and then quit for the day. Practice for a week or two until he's comfortable riding your hand in and out of his cage.

GOOD TRAINING TREATS

Everyone – people or birds – works better when there is a reward involved. For people, the reward might be praise and a paycheck. For your bird, the reward should be praise and a good treat. However, to be a treat it must be something your bird really likes, so you may have to try a few different things until you find a treat your bird gets excited over – maybe shelled sunflower seeds, bits of apple, or a piece of cracker. Once you find a treat your bird really enjoys, save it for your training sessions. To get this special treat, he must do something for you.

A treat is only a treat if it's something your bird really likes.

LEARNING HOW TO LEARN

THE LADDER

This exercise is a continuation of the "up" command. When your bird is out of his cage and comfortable on your hand, place the other hand in the up position in front of his tummy. Tell him "Sweetie, up!" and have him climb onto the index finger of your other hand. When he climbs up and sits there calmly, praise him and offer him a treat. Practice this two or three times and then stop for a bit. A little while later, do it again two or three times. This exercise teaches your bird to step up on either hand and it reinforces the "up" command. Eventually, over time and with practice, you can ask your bird to step from hand to hand – or climb the ladder – up to ten times in a row per training session.

In addition, you will be offering treats to your bird, which is in itself a new skill. With the treat as a motivator, your bird basically learns how to learn.

NO BITE!

Birds bite for several reasons, the first of which is out of fear. A new bird may bite when you offer your hand because he doesn't know who you are. Later, your bird may bite if he thinks you're playing a game. If you reach toward him and then pull your hand away as if you're afraid he'll bite, he will! He may bite if he's tired of being handled and you force petting on him. He may also bite if he thinks he's in charge. To avoid this, don't let him perch on your shoulder or on your head. In the wild, the high-ranking birds sit at the top of the tree. So keep his head lower than your shoulders.

If your bird bites, try to figure out what you're doing that is making him bite, because he's doing it for a reason. Then change the situation if you can. In addition, tell your bird "no bite!" when he does, but other than that, don't make a big deal out of it. Many birds, especially the big birds, enjoy a fuss, and if you get angry and scream and holler, they will holler back!

If you're continuing to have biting problems, ask your veterinarian for a referral to a bird behaviorist. He or she can help you change your bird's behavior.

AVIAN AEROBICS

Your bird was designed to fly, and flying is your bird's best means of exercising. If you have a canary or two, or a couple of finches, their wings are not trimmed and their cage should be big enough for them to fly inside it. If you have a budgie, a cockatiel, or a larger bird, your bird's wings are clipped or trimmed. Although this deprives your bird of the ability to fly much, it is also potentially a life-saver. That's because without the ability to fly, your bird cannot escape from you. However, it also makes exercising more difficult. But fear not – you can help your bird fly.

When your bird trusts you and will step up on your finger with no reservations, take him with you to a closed room. Make sure the windows and doors are securely closed. Now tell your bird, "Sweetie, fly!" and quickly lower your hand with the bird on it. As you quickly drop your hand, your bird will probably flap his wings to maintain his balance. When he flaps, praise him, "Good to fly!"

If he flutters off your finger, have him step back up and try it again. The idea is to teach your bird to grip your finger while he vigorously flaps his wings. This is good, vigorous, aerobic exercise for him.

Later, as he gets better, you may be able to increase the scope of the game. I've seen bird owners actually run through the house with hand upraised and a flapping bird gripping one finger. It may look ridiculous, but both bird and owner were having a great time!

FUN AND SAFE TOYS

You are the most important thing in your bird's life, but you can't spend all day, every day, amusing your bird. Toys can help alleviate his boredom when you're not around. In addition, toys can give your bird a reason to move around, to exercise, and to play.

CHEW TOYS

These are made to be destroyed and are usually wood, rawhide, sisal, acrylic, or even a piece of lava rock. Often you can find a variety of these toys strung together on a rope or wire, so you can hang them from the top of the cage or clip them to a side bar. The bird can manipulate the toys, twirl them with his beak and tongue, and chew on them.

GRASPING TOYS

These are toys that the bird can hold on to with one foot while chewing on them. These are often balsa wood or seed treats molded into a stick shape.

ACTION TOYS

These toys are designed to make your bird move around. One of the most popular exercise toys is a series of rings hung from the top of the cage with a bell or toy hanging from the bottom. The rings should be large enough for your bird to climb all the way through. The way the rings hang together can make climbing through them a challenge. These come in sizes for budgies through to larger parrots. Other action toys include knotted ropes and wooden ladders.

PUZZLE TOYS

These toys are designed to make your bird think. Usually they consist of a treat inside some kind of a puzzle. Your bird can see the treat but must work to get it out. One type has a clear lid over a dish. The treats are in the dish and the bird can see them but he can't eat the treats until he figures out how to open the hinged lid.

PREENING TOYS
These toys encourage the bird to preen them, as he would another bird in his flock. Some of these are made out of sisal or feathers.

MIRRORS
Some birds, especially canaries, finches, and budgies, like mirrors. A small mirror with a few small bells hanging off it are fine for these little birds.

STICKS AND TWIGS
Clean sticks (with no pesticides) can be fun for smaller birds to climb on and explore, and make good chew toys for larger birds.

TOYS TO AVOID
Avoid sharp, brittle plastic toys that are easily broken. Stay away from toys that have lead weights in the bottom. These are both dangerous. Make sure the toy is appropriate for your bird. Don't give a small mirror toy made for budgies to an Amazon parrot; it will be broken and shattered and could hurt your bird.

Don't clutter up your bird's cage with several toys, either. Give your bird one or two toys at a time, and rotate them. Too many toys all the time is like a young child with a room full of toys who tells his mom he doesn't have anything to play with! You can change toys each morning while you clean food dishes. That way your bird will maintain an interest in his toys, and things will seem perpetually new.

PLAY WITH YOUR BIRD
Toys are not just for amusing your bird in his cage. Both of you can play with them. With your bird in his cage, on your finger, or on the playgym, hold one of the toys and invite your bird to investigate it. Let him grab one end while you hold it, or hold it while he chews on the other end. Let your bird climb on a stick while you turn the toy upside down or rotate it. And don't be afraid to laugh while playing with your bird. He will react positively to the higher pitched sounds and won't be offended that you laughed at him. Laughter is good for you and makes playing with your bird a lot more fun.

TIME ON THE PLAYGYM

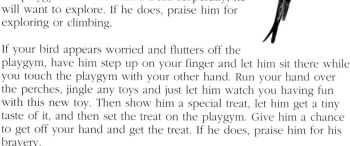

Introduce your bird to a new playgym gradually. When the bird is sitting on your finger, take him to the playgym and let him look at it. If he doesn't appear worried, set him on a perch on the playgym and offer him a treat. Hopefully, he will want to explore. If he does, praise him for exploring or climbing.

If your bird appears worried and flutters off the playgym, have him step up on your finger and let him sit there while you touch the playgym with your other hand. Run your hand over the perches, jingle any toys and just let him watch you having fun with this new toy. Then show him a special treat, let him get a tiny taste of it, and then set the treat on the playgym. Give him a chance to get off your hand and get the treat. If he does, praise him for his bravery.

Most playgyms have a place for food and water dishes. Put some good treats in the food cup and let your bird discover them there. A few tasty treats and he'll lose and fears about this new contraption!

When your bird is comfortable on the playgym, you can let him amuse himself there, climbing and playing with some toys, or you can use this time to play with your bird. With a treat in your hand, encourage him to climb up the playgym, or down, while you teach him "Climb up" or "Climb down." Teach him to sit on a swinging perch hanging on the playgym, or to climb through the hanging rings. Don't be afraid to be silly and have fun.

A playgym offers good exercise for your bird. Climbing up ladders and around on rings or perches will strengthen the muscles in his legs and his jaws (birds use their beaks to help them climb). Swinging will also encourage him to flap his wings to maintain his balance.

You can also use your bird's time on the playgym to introduce new toys, new foods, or new treats. After all, time on the playgym is fun time, so anything introduced there is bound to be fun, right? Your bird may be less picky about foods and treats introduced there than he is about things that are introduced in his cage.

Remember to clean the playgym as often as you clean your bird's cage. That includes putting a fresh piece of newspaper on the floor every day. And make sure to keep the water and food cups clean, too.

When you're choosing a playgym, pick one that will work for you (attached to the cage, set on a table, or on a freestanding perch) and is the right size for your bird. Make sure, too, that it is easily cleaned, wither with a pull-out tray or designed so it it easy to wash.

BIRD BODY LANGUAGE

Birds communicate with each other quite
well, and this communication begins
in the nest when the hatchlings beg for
food from their parents. Your bird tries to
communicate with you, too, except that people often
don't respond correctly. Do you know why your bird bobs his head
at you? Why does he chirp or cluck when you do certain things? The
more you understand, the easier it will be for you to get along with
your bird. Here's a little dictionary.

**Regurgitating, along with head bobbing and moving neck
muscles:** Your bird is saying, "I want to feed you!" This means
you're a favorite person and he wants to give you a very special
present. Birds regurgitate to their young and mates, so this is a very
special gift.

Wiping his beak on the perch: Nothing special, his beak is just
dirty.

Preening: Your bird is cleaning himself, but he only does it when
and where he's comfortable and secure. If he preens you, that's really
special. He likes you!

Fluffing and shaking feathers: Your bird is simply re-arranging his
feathers; perhaps you petted him and messed things up! Or he just
woke up and needed the equivalent of a brushing.

Slapping both wings against his back: This isn't the time to trim
his nails or beak, since he's saying, "Give me some space, please."

Tail feathers spread wide open: He's feeling strong emotions. He
could be happy, but he could also be angry.

Tail twitching from side to side: This bird is happy!

Head lowered and bent, feathers fluffed up on his neck: "Please
scratch my neck!"

Feather pulling or picking: This is a sure sign of stress and must be taken seriously. Some birds will de-nude themselves.

Feed me: If your bird lowers his body position to horizontal with his wings slightly away from his body and shakes as he stares at you while you eat, he's begging. He would like a bite of what you're eating. Hatchlings beg for food from their parents, and grown-up birds will continue this behavior with their owners as long as it achieves results. You can introduce a new food to your bird when he's begging, and he's more apt to try it. You can also use this begging behavior to teach your bird to do some tricks.

Vocalizing: Birds can be very vocal. They vocalize to each other, and they learn it often gets responses from you, too. Most birds call, sing or squawk in the morning, especially when you first take the cover off the cage. Most call loudly when you mist them or give them a shower. Many chirp or call during feeding time. Some will sing along with music.

You can learn a lot more about your bird's ability to communicate by simply watching and listening to him. What does he do when you feed him? What does he do when you mist him or give him a shower? Do you react to any of his body language? For example, do you just know, intuitively, when your bird wants to come out of his cage? You are probably reading his body language and aren't even aware of it.

DAILY CHORES

Your bird cannot clean up after himself. In the wild, he would flit from tree to tree over a large territory, and birdie messes just wouldn't be an issue. But they are in your home.

Unfortunately, he may foul his food and water with feces. This doesn't mean he's stupid – he isn't – it's just that Mother Nature designed him to fly away from his messes. Since he can't, it's your responsibility to maintain a clean environment for him.

SET UP A ROUTINE
The easiest way to take care of the housekeeping chores is to set up a schedule and maintain that routine. Your bird is very much a creature of habit anyway, and will feel comfortable with a routine. The following chores should be done every day.

WASH THE DISHES
All food and water dishes should be removed from the cage and playgym, emptied, and washed thoroughly. Your bird will drop feces in his dishes and cannot be expected to eat food or drink water that is dirty. In addition, bacteria builds up quickly in water fouled by feces.

Many bird owners have two sets of dishes so that one set can be used while the other set is being washed. To clean the dishes, wash them first with dish soap and hot water, using a sponge set aside just for the bird dishes. (Do not use the kitchen sink and the sponge you use to wipe the counters or do the dishes!) Then soak the bird's dishes in a bleach and hot water solution (one cup of bleach to a gallon of hot water is fine) for at least fifteen minutes. Rinse thoroughly, let the dishes air dry, and then refill them and give back to your bird.

REPLACE THE CAGE PAPER

Do you use newspaper or paper towels to line the bottom of your bird's cage? All of the scattered food and dropped feces are caught by the papers on the bottom of the cage, the playgym and the freestanding perch. These must be picked up and removed each day. In the wild birds will forage on the ground, and you don't want your bird foraging for

FEATHERS AND SEED HULLS

Feathers and seed hulls (shells) are the bane of every bird owner. Feathers drift everywhere! It's amazing, too, how far seed hulls can be spread away from the cage. To maintain an illusion of cleanliness around bird cages, I keep a cordless handheld vacuum near the cages. Most come with some mounting hardware so they can be kept right next to the cage. As you walk by and see a mess, you can grab the vacuum, suck up the mess, put the vacuum back and continue on your way. It may take only a minute or two at the most.

dropped food among his feces. Many bird owners will place several layers of paper on the cage bottom and then can pick up one layer each day. This is fine, as long as the remaining papers are clean.

WEEKLY CHORES

The following chores should be done each and every week.

CLEAN THE PERCHES

Your bird will occasionally miss when defecating, and feces may fall on his perches. In addition, when he's hopping around on the bottom of the cage his feet may get dirty, and he'll bring that back up to his perches. And if he thinks his beak is dirty, he's going to wipe the food off on his perch. Needless to say, perches get dirty!

Just as you keep a special sponge set aside for dish and cage cleaning, keep a scrubber pad set aside for perch cleaning. Scrub the perches with the scrubber and then let them soak in the water and bleach solution I described on page 41 for at least fifteen minutes. Rinse thoroughly and let the perches air dry.

WASH THE TOYS

Toys get dirty, too. Plastic toys, lava rocks, and other inedible toys can be scrubbed with soap and water, rinsed with the bleach solution, rinsed again, and dried. Toys meant to be eaten should be thrown away if they get too dirty. Don't soak anything in bleach (or soap) if it's made for your bird to eat.

SCRUB THE CAGE

The cage should be emptied of all its furnishing (dishes, perches, and toys) and either taken outside to the hose or inside to the shower. Rinse it off with running water, then scrub it down with soap and water using the scrubber pad. Splash the bleach and water solution over the cage (making sure not to splash it on yourself or in your eyes). Get bleach into all the corners and crannies of the cage. Let the solution sit for a few minutes, then rinse the cage thoroughly, until you cannot smell the bleach anymore. Let it air dry and then put it all back together again.

CLEAN THE PLAYGYM AND FREESTANDING PERCH

The playgym and perch can be cleaned the way you clean the cage. Take them outside to the hose or back to the shower, scrub them thoroughly, splash them with the bleach solution and rinse. Replace the papers on the bottom.

CLEANING EMERGENCIES

If things get dirty, don't wait until the regularly scheduled day for cleaning – do it right away. For example, if you give your bird some ripe avocado and he wipes his beak all over the perches of his cage, take those perches out and scrub them. It will be a lot easier to get them clean now than to wait until the fruit has dried on and has attracted feathers and feces.

A quick rinse is not enough to get your bird's cage clean. Scrub every inch of the cage thoroughly to make sure all old food, feces, and feathers are removed. Scrub all the trays, toys, perches, and dishes just as carefully.

BIRD BATHS

Have you watched the wild birds in
your backyard enjoy the water from your
lawn sprinklers? They have a great time
ducking into the water, splashing, and
chirping. Birds bathe to rinse off dirt and
dust, to discourage parasites, and to stimulate
preening. Your pet bird needs to bathe, too. Most birds can get by
with a bath twice a week, but some will only preen thoroughly after
a bath; these birds need to bathe more often.

For smaller birds, remove the food bowls from the cage and place
a shallow bowl or saucer of water on the floor of the cage. Fill it
with lukewarm water. Then gently mist your bird with
lukewarm water from a spray bottle.

For medium size birds, use a slightly deeper bowl. Or you
can put the bowl on the bottom of the bathtub or sink and
mist your bird there. Let him splash and play in the bowl while
you mist him. You can also let him play with the water running out
of the faucet, but keep checking the water temperature to make sure
it doesn't get too hot or too cold.

For larger birds, you can take the bird into the shower with you.
Don't use soap or shampoo on him, of course, and don't keep the
water too hot, but let him play in it. Place him on the shower curtain
rod when he's done and then you can finish your shower.

HOW TO HOLD YOUR BIRD

You don't need to hold your bird for a bath, but you will for other
grooming procedures. Birds rarely like to be restrained. After all, a
bird that is caught is prey! However, you need to be able to hold
your bird to care for him, and ideally you should be able to do this
without stressing your bird too much. Make your move calmly,
swiftly, and surely, and your bird will soon settle down.

CANARIES, FINCHES, AND OTHER SMALL BIRDS

If your bird's wings are not clipped, or if your small bird is not finger
trained, catch him using this method. Take all of the furnishings out

of his cage, including perches and dishes. With a small towel or washcloth over your hand, corner him in the bottom of the cage and flip the washcloth over him. Before he escapes, grab him so that his back is toward the palm of your hand, his legs are forward, and his head is between your thumb and index finger.

BUDGIES AND COCKATIELS

If your bird is finger trained and his wings have been clipped, take him out of his cage on your finger. With your other hand, grasp him firmly but carefully from behind so that his back is in the palm of your hand and his feet are forward. If he is trying to bite you, place your thumb on one side of his head near the beak and your index finger on the other side of his head.

LARGER BIRDS

Use a larger towel, and concentrate on controlling your bird's head. Although smaller birds are certainly capable of biting, a bite from an angry budgie is significantly less painful than a bite from an angry macaw!

Whenever you're holding your bird, make sure most of the gripping pressure is on the bird's sides rather than his chest. Birds are fragile, and too much pressure on the chest will make a bird stop breathing. Make sure, too, that his wings are folded into your hand or under the towel properly. Don't use pressure to hold him if the wings are out of alignment; you could break some bones or feathers if you do.

NAILS AND WINGS

If your bird's toenails are so sharp that they hurt you, or if his nails are so long that he has trouble grasping a perch properly, they need to be trimmed.

TRIMMING TOENAILS

Birds' toenails grow continuously, just as your own nails do. Your bird will wear his nails down a little bit through normal activity, especially if he has a concrete perch or two in his cage or on his playgym. However, his nails still usually have to be trimmed. Nails left to grow too long can deform your bird's feet and, in extreme cases, can actually grow in a circle back into the foot.

The toenails of small birds can be trimmed using nail clippers made for people, while larger birds can be trimmed with nail clippers made for dogs. In either case, make sure the blade is sharp; you want to cut the nail, not crush it. Make sure you have some styptic powder (such as Qik-Stop) on hand just in case you nick a blood vessel.

If you are right-handed, hold the bird in your left hand. If you need to, hold the bird wrapped in a towel. Bring one foot out of the towel at a time. If your bird has light colored nails, you will be able to see the quick (the pink part where the blood vessels are). If you cut into the quick it will hurt, your bird will panic, and the nail will bleed. Don't cut into the quick! With these light colored nails, just quickly trim each nail a little bit, making sure to leave some nail over the end of the quick.

With dark colored nails, take just a tiny bit off one nail until you see the tiniest bit of blood. Pack it with styptic powder and cut all the other nails just a little bit longer than that one. When one foot is done, do the other one the same way.

Trimming your bird's wings really isn't difficult if you have someone to help you hold your bird. But if you're worried about doing it right, ask your veterinarian to show you how. Watch carefully, and don;t be afraid to ask questions.

CLIPPING WINGS

Clipping the wings involves trimming the flight feathers so that your bird can flutter but not fly. This allows you to give him some freedom outside of his cage without being too worried about the bird escaping or flying away. It will also protect him from flying hard into walls or windows. Cutting the feathers properly causes the bird no pain, although many birds dislike being restrained.

It's much easier to trim the wings with another person helping you. Have your helper hold your bird, using the techniques I described on page 45. Gently stretch out one wing. Using very sharp scissors, trim the first several flight feathers (the longer ones farthest from the wing bone itself), beginning at the wing tip. Cut the feathers about halfway down. For budgies, trim five to six feathers. On cockatiels, trim seven to eight feathers. Larger birds can get by with only five to six feathers trimmed.

When you have finished trimming one wing, fold that wing back up, extend the other wing, and do the same thing.

When trimming the wings, look carefully for new feathers growing in. Blood feathers (new ones) will still have a keratin sheath over them – they will look different. Make sure you don't cut these new feathers, because they will bleed, sometimes quite heavily. If you accidentally cut one of these blood feathers, grasp the feather close to the skin with tweezers and pull it out. With a gauze pad, put pressure on the wound (it may ooze blood) and hold your bird still for several minutes so that he can't flap and cause it to bleed again.

A HEALTHY BEAK

The beak is a versatile tool for your bird. He uses it to grab, climb, eat, grip, grind, and groom. The beak is made of hollow bone, with sinuses on the inside and a thin layer of keratin on the outside.

A bird's beak is a tool for grasping and climbing as well as eating.

Your bird's overall health depends upon a healthy beak. If the beak is damaged, overgrown or otherwise impaired, your bird will have difficulty eating. In addition, he could have trouble moving around because when birds climb, they reach up and grab with their beak first, followed by their feet. It's very important to keep a close eye on your bird's beak.

The beak constantly grows because it is constantly worn down. Most birds keep their beak worn down to a good length by eating, chewing on the cuttlebone in their cage, chewing on a mineral block, and using their beak to play with toys. However, if your bird has a beak that is slightly crooked (the way some people have crooked teeth), the beak may not wear down evenly or may grow unevenly. If your bird is inactive – not playing enough or not using his chew toys – he may not keep the beak in correct trim, either. And some birds have good beaks and are very active but still have overgrown beaks. That happens when the upper and lower jaws are not perfectly aligned.

SPOTTING A PROBLEM

When the top of the beak is overgrown, it will appear to be too long. Your bird may try to pick things up from the side of his beak rather than with the front of it. If the bottom beak is too long, your bird may not be able to close his beak and may appear to be panting. The lower beak may also grow or curve to one side. When the beak is overgrown, or if it has a tendency to overgrow, regular trimming will be needed to keep the beak at the proper size and length.

TRIMMING THE BEAK

If you've never trimmed a bird's beak, take your bird to a veterinarian and let him or her show you how to do it correctly. The beak has nerves and a blood supply, and if the trimming is done incorrectly you could hurt your bird and could also deform his beak.

KEEP YOUR BIRD'S BEAK HEALTHY BY FOLLOWING THESE SUGGESTIONS:

• Feed him a good diet so your bird has the right nutrition to grow a healthy beak.

• Offer cuttlebones or mineral blocks made for birds to provide something to chew on, as well as a source of calcium and minerals.

• Provide chewing toys, such as perches made of sticks or concrete, and attractive toys that your bird wants to play with.

• Provide opportunities for your bird to climb, creating a chance for him to use his beak.

A cuttlebone is the bone of a cuttlefish – a relative of the squid. It is fine right from the store for budgies, cockatiels and larger birds. But it's a bit too salty for the little songbirds. For them, soak the bone in water overnight and let it dry before you clip it to the cage.

THE AVIAN VETERINARIAN

You should bring your new bird in to meet the veterinarian within the first day or two after he comes home. Although this will be a stressful visit, your vet should be able to meet your bird, examine him, and establish his health status. The vet will look for any obvious signs of disease, as well as any genetic health defects. He or she will also check for parasites, including feather mites, lice, and other noxious critters! If your veterinarian does find a problem, he or she can advise you on how to deal with it. In addition, at this visit the vet can trim your bird's nails and wings and show you how to do it.

During your first visit, you can also ask the vet any questions you might have. What should your bird's feces look like and how often will he eliminate? What does it mean when he fluffs up his feathers? This is the time to ask any of those questions you have been wondering about.

During your first visit, your vet may want to analyze your bird's droppings to check for parasites, and may also want to do a blood work-up. Although this may seem extreme for a bird who looks healthy, it's really not a bad idea. If there are any hidden problems lurking in your bird's system, these tests will find them. And if it turns out that your bird is healthy, these tests can serve as a baseline later if your bird becomes sick. Your vet will have a "normal" to compare future tests against.

ANNUAL CHECK-UPS

An annual visit is just as important as the first visit, and for the same reasons. In the wild, a bird who gives clues that he is injured or ill will be singled out by predators. In captivity, your bird has retained those instincts, and they make it much harder for bird owners to determine whether or not their bird is sick. An annual check-up, complete with blood and fecal tests, can often detect hidden problems.

FINDING A BIRD DOCTOR

Birds are very special, very fragile creatures, and your bird needs a veterinarian who understands just how special he is. An avian veterinarian will know about bird diseases, how to treat injuries and what medications are useful for birds. The veterinary office where you take your dog and cat may be able to refer you to a veterinarian who specializes in birds. You can also ask for referrals from other bird owners or from pet shops that specialize in birds.

If you're having trouble finding an avian vet in your area, contact the Association of Avian Veterinarians for a referral. Their address is PO Box 811720, Boca Raton, FL 33481-1720, phone (561) 393-8901, or www.aav.org.

Your avian veterinarian can show you how to trim your bird's wings and nails. He or she can also tell you about the best diet for your type of bird, and any other special requirements your bird might have. These finches, or example, need extra light and heat in the winter.

SIGNS OF HEALTH

All healthy birds share some characteristics, although they may vary slightly from bird to bird, or among different types of birds. What is most important is that you learn what is normal for your bird.

- **EYES:** Bright, shiny, clear, with no discharge and no cloudiness
- **CERE:** Clean and dry, with no discharge
- **RESPIRATION:** Breaths should move in and out cleanly
- **BEAK:** Should appear strong with no crusted food, no discharge or drooling
- **SKIN:** Clear and clean under the feathers
- **FEATHERS:** Healthy, shiny, laying flat
- **FEET:** Clean and dry, skin is clear
- **FECES:** Normal, no changes
- **WEIGHT:** Normal, flesh over bones, not too light nor too heavy
- **ATTITUDE:** Alert, watchful, ready to do and explore
- **ENERGY LEVEL:** Depends upon type of bird and age; ready to go, ready to sing, talk, or play

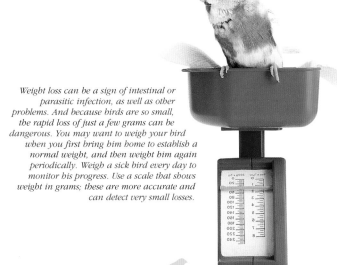

Weight loss can be a sign of intestinal or parasitic infection, as well as other problems. And because birds are so small, the rapid loss of just a few grams can be dangerous. You may want to weigh your bird when you first bring him home to establish a normal weight, and then weight him again periodically. Weigh a sick bird every day to monitor his progress. Use a scale that shows weight in grams; these are more accurate and can detect very small losses.

SIGNS OF ILLNESS

Birds are delicate animals and can fade very quickly. If you see any of the following early signs of illness, get in touch with your avian veterinarian right away.

- **EYES:** Matter or discharge, cloudy, closed or partially closed
- **CERE:** Discharge, crusted
- **RESPIRATION:** Panting, wheezing, audible breathing
- **BEAK:** Cracked, broken, crusty matter adhering to it, drooling
- **SKIN:** Red, inflamed, crusty, scabby
- **FEATHERS:** Unseasonal or extra heavy molting, unhealthy or scraggly feathers, bald spots
- **FEET:** Red, inflamed, crusty, obviously sore
- **FECES:** Any change from normal, blood in feces, mucus, feces and matted feathers around the vent
- **WEIGHT:** Abrupt drop in weight, lack of appetite, increased eating of grit
- **ATTITUDE:** Change in posture, hunched up, head down or pulled in, feathers fluffed up, no interest in surroundings, no desire to come out of the cage
- **ENERGY LEVEL:** Any unexplained change from normal, lethargic, passive

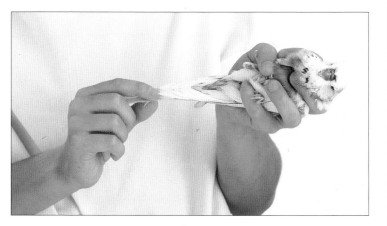

BIRD EMERGENCIES

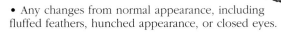

Make an appointment to see your
veterinarian as soon as possible if you
see any of the following.

• Any changes in the bird's normal attitude,
even if there are no other obvious
symptoms.

• Any changes from normal appearance, including
fluffed feathers, hunched appearance, or closed eyes.

• Any changes in normal eating or drinking habits, even if there are
no other obvious symptoms.

• Depending on whether or not you've fed your bird a new food,
any changes in the bird's feces. Loose, running, unformed, discolored
feces.

You have an emergency if any of the following happen. Get your
bird to a veterinarian immediately.

• Your bird has trouble breathing, including sneezing, panting,
wheezing; breathing through the mouth and
breathing while holding onto a cage bar with his
neck extended.

• Your bird is injured by another bird or
an animal.

• Your bird has been exposed to, eaten, or
inhaled something toxic. This includes smoke
from nonstick cookware, which is highly toxic
to birds.

• Your bird has been burned either by heat or by
exposure to caustic chemicals.

• Your bird has been injured and is bleeding.

YOUR BIRD'S FIRST AID KIT

❐ Gauze pads

❐ Tape

❐ Hydrogen peroxide

❐ Antibiotic ointment

❐ Pepto bismol and/or Kaopectate

❐ Rolls of gauze of different widths

❐ Honey or Karo syrup for hypoglycemia

❐ Scissors; round tip and sharp blades

❐ Plastic eye dropper for liquids

❐ Styptic pencil or powder

❐ Needlenose pliers or tweezers to remove a nicked bloodfeather

❐ Nail clippers

❐ Towel for restraining bird

❐ An incandescent lamp with a working bulb and an extension cord to keep the bird warm

EMERGENCY FIRST AID

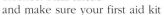

Birds can be incredibly
fragile, and in an
emergency time is
always of the
essence. Plan ahead
and make sure your first aid kit
is always handy. Make sure, too, that you have your veterinarian's
phone number, beeper number, and the emergency bird clinic's
number. Put the numbers in the first aid kit, beside your phone, and
in your wallet. Your bird's best chance for survival in an emergency is
to get to the veterinarian quickly. But there are some things you can
do before you get there to help him out.

WARMTH

The most important thing you can do for a sick bird is to keep him
warm. In any bird emergency, make sure you keep your bird warm
while you get him to the veterinarian. A temperature of eighty to
ninety degrees Fahrenheit is ideal. Use a thermometer to make sure
it's not too hot or too cold.

When you heat a cage, make sure you leave an unheated area that
your bird can move to if he feels too hot. For small cages, such as
the kind you might use to transport your bird, place a heating pad or
a hot water bottle beneath the cage or alongside it. To prevent heat
loss, cover the cage on the top and three sides with a towel. A small
aquarium with a screen or towel for a roof also makes a good
hospital cage. Place a heating pad under one side of the aquarium.

BLEEDING

Use gauze pads to put direct pressure on the wound. When bleeding
stops, use hydrogen peroxide to wash the wound, followed by
antibiotic ointment. Get the bird to the veterinarian right away to
prevent shock from setting in.

SHOCK

If your bird has been injured or has been badly frightened, he may
go into shock. Keep him warm, offer him some electrolyte solution

(such as Gatorade or Pedialyte) by eyedropper and get him to the vet's office right away. This is always life-threatening.

BROKEN BONES

If your bid perches on one leg while holding a leg up or allowing a leg to droop, or if one wing is hanging, he has probably broken a bone. Move the bird as little as possible. Don't try to set or splint the limb – just get him to the vet's office right away.

EGG BINDING

If your female bird is squatting on the floor of the cage, has a swollen abdomen and is straining, she's probably trying to pass an egg and is having trouble (girls will sometimes lay eggs even when there are no boys around – the eggs just won't hatch). Keep her warm (up to eighty-five degrees), offer her some Gatorade by eye dropper, and dampen her vent area with warm water. If she doesn't pass the egg within an hour, take her to your vet.

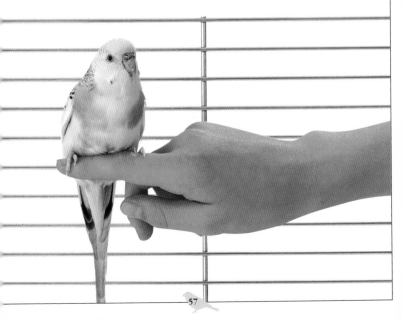

YOUR BIRD NEEDS YOU

Birds are very social creatures. In the
wild they live in flocks or in pairs.
Many birds bond for life
and grieve horribly when
they lose a mate.
There's no question
that birds have feelings.
In captivity, your bird needs your time,
attention, and affection. A bird that feels neglected rarely thrives,
and many actually die.

Dr. Irene Pepperberg at the University of Arizona has been working
since 1977 with an amazing African grey parrot named Alex. Alex can
sort and indicate objects by their shape, color, and texture. When Dr.
Pepperberg presents him with a tray full of objects and asks, "Find the
green, round, fuzzy thing," he can! Alex can also count, tell you what
he wants to eat, and talk about how he is feeling. Clearly, he is using
language in context and not just mimicking words he has been taught.

Many bird owners report that their birds also use language in context.
And there's no reason to believe that birds who lack the ability to
mimic human speech aren't equally smart – they just can't talk about
it! The more we know about avian intelligence, the more we
understand that birds need plenty of time spent interacting with us.

Keeping your bird's cage in a part of the house where there is often
activity is fine, as long as people still pay direct attention to the bird.
If you work at home, put your bird's cage (or
his playgym or freestanding perch) in your
home office. Watch, listen, and pay attention
to your bird. What do his chirps, clucks,
and trills mean? Try to mimic him and see
what he does. Watch his body language;
what is he doing and why?

Take the time to do things with your bird, to train him and to socialize him, to play with him and to teach him tricks. Some of the best time spent with him can also be your quiet times; just hold him and cuddle with him while you're reading or watching television.

Birds were not meant to spend their entire lives in cages. If you try to turn your bird into an ornament, he will grow deeply depressed. But when you invite your bird into your flock, he'll be the most entertaining, amusing, loving friend you can imagine.

As I write this, Pretty Bird, my cockatiel, is on my desk clucking to himself as he rips up some scrap papers. When he gets bored with that, he'll go over to his windowsill perch next to my desk and watch the wild birds outside at their feeder.

I treasure this time with my bird because I think I see more of his real personality when he's outside of his cage. He can explore (within certain limits, of course), play, talk to me (in his own language!) and when he wants to, he can cuddle with me. In fact, he's smart enough to have learned that although I don't stop working at the computer for many things, if he wants to come up and cuddle (which he signals by climbing onto the front of my shirt under my chin), I will stop work to cuddle him. Smart bird!

MORE TO LEARN

BOOKS

The Complete Bird Owner's Handbook, by Gary Gallerstein, DVM, Howell Book House

The Complete Book of Cockatiels, by Diane Grindol, Howell Book House

The Consumer's Guide to Feeding Birds, by Liz Palika, Howell Book House

The Everything Bird Book, by Tershia d'Elgin, Adams Media

Guide to a Well-Behaved Parrot, by Mattie Sue Athan, Barron's Educational Series

The Pleasure of Their Company: An Owner's Guide to Parrot Training, by Bonnie Munro Doane, Howell Book House

101 Essential Tips: Caring for Your Pet Bird, Dorling Kindersley Publishing

MAGAZINES

Bird Talk
PO Box 6050
Mission Viejo, CA 92690
(714) 855-8822
www.birdtalk.com

Bird Times
7-L Dundas Circle
Greensboro, NC 27407
(336) 292-4047
www.birdtimes.com

NATIONAL BIRD CLUBS

American Budgerigar Society
1600 W. Meadow Lane
Visalia, CA 93277
(209) 734-5992
absec@lightspeed.net

American Canary Fanciers
Association
2020 Kew Dr.
Los Angeles, CA 90046
(213) 255-2679

American Cockatiel Society
9527 60th Lane N.
Pinellas Park, FL 34666
www.acstiels.com

Bird Clubs of America
PO Box 2005
Yorktown, VA 23692
(757) 898-5090
www.oldstone.com/bca.htm

National Cage Bird Show Club
4910 Anthony Lane
Pasadena, TX 77504
www.ncbs.org

National Finch and Softbill
Society
PO Box 3232
Ballwin, MO 63022
(314) 394-3530
www.geocities.com/~NFSSnet/

WEB SITES

Alternative Veterinary Medicine
www.altvetmed.com

American Animal Hospital
Association
www.healthypet.com

American Veterinary Medical
Association
www.avma.org/care4pets

Me and My Budgie
www.budgies.org

NetVet
www.avma.org/netvet/cats.htm

Up at Six Aviaries
www.upatsix.com

ABOUT THE AUTHOR

Liz Palika and her husband Paul share their home with a
variety of pets. They have owned lovebirds, budgies,
cockatiels, African greys, and a lesser sulfur crested cockatoo,
as well as dogs, cats, and reptiles. Liz has written many
award-winning books on animal care and training, including
The Consumer's Guide to Feeding Birds.

INDEX

Dorling DK Kindersley

LONDON, NEW YORK, SYDNEY, DELHI, PARIS,
MUNICH, JOHANNESBURG

Project Editor: Beth Adelman
Design: Carol Wells
Cover Design: Gus Yoo
Photo Research: Mark Dennis, Martin Copeland
Index: Nanette Cardon

Photo Credits: Paul Bricknell, Cyril Chadwick, Frank Greenaway,
Cyril Laubscher

First American Edition, 2000
2 4 6 8 10 9 7 5 3 1

Published in the United States by
Dorling Kindersley Publishing, Inc. 95 Madison Avenue New York, New York 10016

Dorling Kindersley Publishing, Inc. offers special discounts for bulk purchases for sales promotion or premiums. Specific, large-quantity needs can be met with special editions, including personalized covers, excerpts of existing guides, and corporate imprints. For more information, contact Special Markets Department, Dorling Kindersley Publishing, Inc.,
95 Madison Avenue, New York, NY 10016 Fax: (800) 600-9098.

Color reproduction by Colourscan, Singapore
Printed in Hong Kong by Wing King Tong

Library of Congress Cataloging-in-Publication Data
Palika, Liz, 1954-
    What your bird needs / Liz Palika.-- 1st American ed.
       p. cm. -- (What your pet needs)
Includes index.
    ISBN 0-7894-6310-5 (alk. paper)
    1. Cage birds. I. Title. II. Series.
SF461 .P15 2000
    636.6'8--dc21
00-008257

LP808   155

See our complete catalog at
www.dk.com